Welcome to Vocabulary Power
sound-a-likes

400 homonyms and homophones to know for reading comprehension

knight

night

Available in the Series

back

The tall boy is standing in the **back** of the line.

Please scratch the itch on my **back**.

whine

wine

Mom doesn't like it
when I **whine**.

The waiter poured a glass
of **wine** for each person.

band

The **band** plays music at the country fair.

Use a rubber **band** to hold the papers.

which

Which of these hats would you like to buy?

witch

The **witch** mixed her magic brew.

bank

The girl deposits her money in the **bank**.

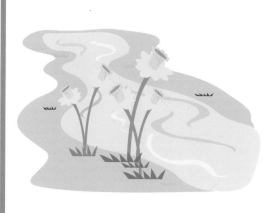

Daffodils grow along the **bank** of the river.

weather

whether

Summer **weather** is hot and humid.

I wonder **whether** I'll have vanilla or chocolate?

bark

A caterpillar is crawling on the **bark** of the tree.

Her terrier has a loud and annoying **bark**.

wear

I want to **wear** my flip-flops to the beach.

where

Where is my pet turtle hiding?

bat

The **bat** flew into the dark cave.

He hit a home run with his brand-new **bat**.

weak

The elderly man was
frail and **weak**.

week

School vacation begins
in one **week**.

batter

Add some chocolate chips to the cake **batter**.

The pitcher throws the ball to the **batter**.

way

It is a long **way** to the moon.

weigh

How much does an elephant **weigh**?

bed

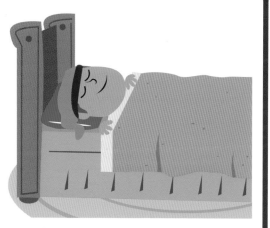

Grandpa is snoring
in his cozy **bed**.

Look at the colorful
bed of flowers.

warn

The sign will **warn** the skaters about thin ice.

worn

My brother's pants are **worn** at the knees.

block

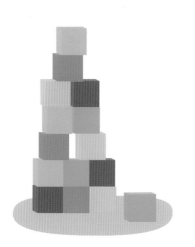

Carefully place one more **block** on top of the tower.

Block the kick so he doesn't score.

wait

I have to **wait** to see the dentist.

weight

The doctor checks the baby's **weight**.

blue

The jumbo jet soars across the **blue** sky.

She feels **blue** because her necklace broke.

waist

He buckled the leather belt around his **waist**.

waste

Don't dump the **waste** into the river.

bowl

This is a delicious **bowl** of ice cream.

Our team likes to **bowl** on Wednesday nights.

wail

whale

My sister begins to **wail** when she is hungry.

The blue **whale** travels great distances for food.

cap

Put the **cap** on the tube of toothpaste.

He wears a red **cap** to the baseball game.

vane

The weather **vane** shows the direction of the wind.

vein

I can see the bulging **vein** on the old man's hand.

cast

He needs a **cast** for his broken arm.

The actor auditions to be in the **cast**.

toad

towed

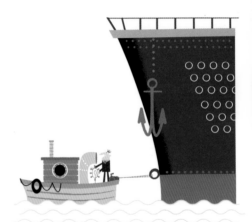

A green **toad** was hiding under the rock.

The tugboat **towed** the ship to the port.

channel

We changed the **channel** to see the cartoons.

The athlete swam across the English **Channel**.

tide

The high **tide** washed away our sand castle.

tied

She **tied** a yellow bow in her hair.

check

Mom wrote a **check** to pay for the groceries.

Check your homework before you hand it in.

throne

thrown

The queen sat on the
royal **throne**.

The football was **thrown**
by the quarterback.

Pirates found a treasure **chest** on the island.

The weight lifter has a muscular **chest**.

threw

through

The garbage man **threw** the trash into the truck.

He walked **through** the turnstile to the train.

China is one of the largest countries.

My mother's new **china** is very fragile.

their

They took **their** coats when they left the house.

there

Hang the picture over **there** by the piano.

coach

The princess rode in an elegant **coach**.

The baseball team listened to their **coach**.

teas

There are a variety of **teas** from around the world.

tease

The bully likes to **tease** the smaller children.

coat

The clown wore a colorful **coat**.

Our fence needs a new **coat** of paint.

tear

Cutting the onion made
my eyes **tear**.

tier

We sat in the upper **tier**
of the theater.

crane

The **crane** lifted the lumber to the top.

Two hikers saw a **crane** wading in the water.

tea

Some people prefer
tea to coffee.

tee

The golfer places the
ball on the **tee**.

ear

The boy shook the water out of his **ear**.

We broke the **ear** of corn off the stalk.

taught

She **taught** us how to use the potter's wheel.

taut

Pull the rope **taut** to secure the boat.

eye

The pirate has a patch on his **eye**.

Put the thread through the **eye** of the needle.

tail

The monkey hung from a branch by its **tail**.

tale

Tell me the **tale** of Jack and the Beanstalk.

fall

The leaves change color in the **fall**.

If you run carelessly, you may **fall**.

tacks

tax

I use **tacks** to hang photos on my board.

Dad pays income **tax** every year.

My **feet** don't fit into my old shoes.

The friendly giant is ten **feet** tall.

sundae

I ordered a hot fudge **sundae** with nuts.

Sunday

My family visited the art museum on **Sunday**.

fence

There were blackbirds
sitting on my **fence**.

The men picked up their
swords to **fence**.

straight

strait

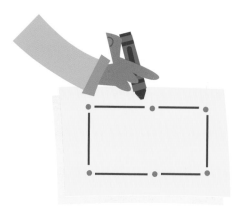

Draw a **straight** line to connect the dots.

The ship passed through the **strait** to the ocean.

file

My secretary put the **file** in the cabinet.

The manicurist will **file** the woman's nails.

steal

The thief tried to **steal** the lady's purse.

steel

Skyscrapers are made with **steel** beams.

fire

A blazing **fire** destroyed the forest.

His boss will **fire** him if he doesn't do his work.

stake

steak

Hammer the **stake** to hold the tent in place.

Let's cook the **steak** on the grill.

fly

A pesky **fly** is bothering the man.

The geese **fly** in a V formation.

stair

She left her toy on the bottom **stair**.

stare

Can you **stare** at me without blinking?

fork

Use a **fork** to eat your dinner.

We came to a **fork** in the road.

son

The father showed his **son** how to fly a kite.

sun

The **sun** rises in the east at dawn.

gum

When I chew **gum**
I blow bubbles.

My brand-new tooth
came through my **gum**.

some

There are **some** jelly beans left in the jar.

sum

$4+5=9$

The **sum** of four plus five is nine.

key

An iron **key** unlocked the treasure chest.

The opera singer sang off-**key**.

soar

Watch the seagull **soar** across the sky.

sore

I stayed in bed because I have a **sore** throat.

lace

The collar of her blouse is made of **lace**.

Don't forget to tie the **lace** on your sneaker.

slay

The brave knight will **slay** the green-eyed dragon.

sleigh

After the snowstorm we went for a **sleigh** ride.

land

A seaplane can **land** on water.

The farmer grows corn on his **land**.

side

Plant the tree on the **side** of the house.

sighed

He **sighed** with relief when he passed the test.

There is no more cereal **left** in the box.

Make a **left** turn at the traffic light.

shoe

shoo

I found my pink **shoe**.

Shoo the flies away from the picnic table.

letter

Use a capital **letter** when you write your name.

I wrote a **letter** to my pen pal.

sew

The seamstress will **sew** the hem of the skirt.

sow

The farmer will **sow** the seeds for the crop.

light

A feather is very **light**.

Turn off the **light** when you leave the room.

sea

The humpback whales swim far out at **sea**.

see

Use your telescope to **see** the stars.

march

JANUARY
FEBRUARY
MARCH

March is the third month of the year.

The musicians **march** in the parade.

scent

The perfume had a
fragrant **scent**.

sent

I **sent** a thank-you note
to my tutor.

mark

He earned the highest **mark** on the test.

The dog's muddy paw made a **mark** on the rug.

sail

Let's hoist the **sail** to catch the wind.

sale

The department store is having a holiday **sale**.

match

My socks don't **match**.

She lit the candle with a **match**.

rose

The groom wore a single **rose** in his lapel.

rows

The farmer planted many **rows** of corn.

This new racing bike is **mine**.

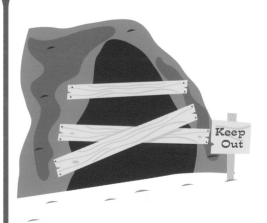

They searched for gold in the abandoned **mine**.

root

The **root** of the tree broke through the sidewalk.

route

Check the map to find the best **route**.

mint

He watched them **mint** the new coins.

I love **mint** chocolate chip ice cream.

role

I have a major **role** in the school play.

roll

The child loves to **roll** down the hill.

The boy is building a **model** plane.

A fashion **model** wears designer clothing.

roe

row

Eggs of a fish are called **roe**.

The beans were planted in a straight **row**.

nail

He used a hammer and **nail** to repair the table.

The witch has a long pointy **nail** on her finger.

road

The winding **road** led
to the mansion.

rode

We **rode** horses
on the beach.

note

Mom wrote a **note** to my teacher.

The singer reached a very high **note**.

ring

My aunt's **ring** fell
down the drain.

wring

The janitor had to
wring out the mop.

order

The waitress took our **order**.

Put the words in alphabetical **order**.

right

100%
ALL CORRECT

All of my answers were **right** on the science test.

write

I'll **write** a letter to my pen pal.

palm

He held a snail in the **palm** of his hand.

Palm trees grow in tropical climates.

read

We must **read** five books
this summer.

reed

I plucked a **reed** from
the river's edge.

park

Park the car next to the curb.

The **park** is a great place for a picnic.

read

red

The author **read** a poem to our class yesterday.

Red rose bushes grew along the fence.

The doctor treated the **patient**.

You have to be **patient** when waiting in line.

rap

The audience gathered to hear the **rap** singer.

wrap

Wrap mom's gift with paper and ribbons.

pen

The author wrote his signature with a **pen**.

Farm animals were enclosed in the **pen**.

rain

Our game was canceled because of **rain**.

reign

The king and queen **reign** over the kingdom.

play

They went to the theater
to see the **play**.

The children **play** ball
in the park.

prince

The **prince** wore
a fancy cape.

prints

The robber carelessly left
his **prints** on the safe.

point

The pencil has a
sharp **point**.

Point to the prize
that you want.

pray

I **pray** every night before I go to bed.

prey

The lion hunts its **prey** in the jungle.

The baker opened a
5-**pound** bag of sugar.

Lost dogs are taken
to the **pound**.

pore

A **pore** is one of the many tiny holes in your skin.

pour

Will you **pour** some iced tea into the glass?

race

Children of every **race** were in the class.

The children participated in the relay **race**.

plain

She chose the **plain** dress for the interview.

plane

The **plane** descended into the airport.

The tennis champion broke her **racket**.

Stray cats made a **racket** in the alley.

pedal

His brother taught him how to **pedal** his bike.

peddle

My great grandfather used to **peddle** his wares.

raise

Will you **raise** my allowance?

They **raise** the flag every morning.

peak

The climbers reached the **peak** of Mount Everest.

peek

Don't **peek** at your birthday presents.

ram

The **ram** has long, curly horns.

A reckless driver might **ram** into the pole.

CAUTION

peace

The generals signed
the **peace** treaty.

piece

This **piece** of apple pie
is delicious.

range

Many years ago buffalo roamed the open **range**.

We scrambled the eggs on the electric **range**.

pair

The hockey player has a new **pair** of skates.

pear

I have a juicy **pear** in my lunch box.

ring

She wore a fancy **ring** on her finger.

I can't hear the phone **ring** when I'm in the shower.

pain

My toothache caused me a lot of **pain**.

pane

The ball crashed through the **pane** of glass.

roll

I ate my sandwich on a
whole wheat **roll**.

The teacher called the
roll in class.

pail

Let's fill the **pail** with sand to make a castle.

pale

The **pale** man is next to the tan lifeguard.

row

I sit in the front **row** of the classroom.

Row the boat across the lake.

one

The salesman sold **one** hat to the lady.

won

The tennis player **won** the tournament.

run

The politician decided to **run** for mayor.

A cheetah can **run** faster than most other animals.

oar

The wooden **oar** slipped into the water.

ore

An old miner finally discovered gold **ore**.

saw

A carpenter uses a **saw** to cut planks of wood.

The girl **saw** a robin on the fence.

muscle

Look at the **muscle**
I can make.

mussel

The seagull cracked open
the **mussel** for his dinner.

The diver observed the **school** of fish.

Our **school** has a new principal.

moose

mousse

The **moose** wandered
through the woods.

Chocolate **mousse** is my
favorite dessert.

shed

Many snakes **shed** their skin every year.

We keep our bicycles in the **shed**.

missed

She **missed** the bus and was late for school.

mist

Morning **mist** clouded the window.

The cruise **ship** sailed into the port.

Let's **ship** the package to Grandma.

meat

The Tyrannosaurus rex was a **meat** eater.

meet

It is polite to shake hands when you **meet** someone.

sink

Place the dirty dishes in the **sink**.

The damaged boat will **sink** to the bottom.

mail

male

The postman carried the **mail** on his back.

A **male** horse is called a stallion.

space

The astronauts traveled through **space**.

There is no more **space** in the closet.

made

We **made** a jack-o'-lantern for Halloween.

maid

The **maid** brought the queen some tea.

spell

My teacher asked me to **spell** the word.

The wicked witch put a **spell** on the prince.

leak

leek

The plumber repaired the **leak** under the sink.

A **leek** is a vegetable that tastes like a sweet onion.

spring

The **spring** popped out of the worn mattress.

Flowers begin to bloom in the early **spring**.

lay

The hen will **lay** her eggs in the morning.

lei

A Hawaiian woman welcomed me with a **lei**.

stand

The violinist placed her music on the **stand**.

I had to **stand** in front of the class.

know

I don't **know** which way to go.

no

The sign means "**No** smoking."

star

The North **Star** shines brightly in the sky.

He is the **star** of the musical show.

knot

not

The fisherman tied a **knot** in the net.

I am **not** going to cross until it turns green.

tag

Check the price **tag** on the scooter.

Let's play **tag** in the school yard.

knight

The **knight** charged
into battle.

night

Owls stay awake
at **night**.

tick

We heard the loud **tick** of the grandfather clock.

I found a **tick** on my dog's neck.

knead

The baker will **knead** the dough for the bread.

need

The traveler will **need** water to cross the desert.

We gave dad a striped **tie** for his birthday.

The bicycle race ended in a **tie**.

in

Dirty clothes are **in** the washing machine.

inn

The country **inn** is at the end of the winding road.

toast

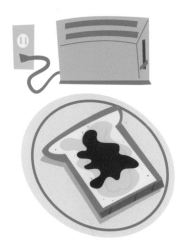

I put butter and jelly on my **toast**.

Dad made a **toast** to the bride and groom.

hour

The alarm clock will wake Dad in one **hour**.

our

Look at **our** new watches.

tongue

My taste buds are on my **tongue**.

Pull the **tongue** of your shoe before you lace it.

hole

The chipmunk dug a **hole** in the ground.

whole

I ate the **whole** bag of chips by myself.

top

They climbed to the **top** of the mountain.

The child tried to spin the **top**.

hoarse

The cheerleader is **hoarse** from shouting.

horse

His **horse** galloped across the range.

track

The train rumbled down the **track**.

Keep **track** of your homework assignments.

him

A waiter brought the food to **him**.

hymn

The choir sang a **hymn** to the congregation.

trip

We are taking a cross-country **trip**.

You might **trip** over your shoelaces.

hi

I said "**Hi**" to everyone
at the party.

high

The track star jumped
over the **high** hurdle.

watch

We'll **watch** the fireworks at the carnival.

I can tell time with my new digital **watch**.

heard

herd

I **heard** music through my headphones.

The cowboys rounded up the **herd** of cattle.

well

My brother is not feeling very **well**.

We threw the coin into the wishing **well**.

hear

The campers **hear** the crickets at night.

here

Let's set up our tent **here**, by the lake.

ad

We placed an **ad** in the newspaper.

add

Add a spoonful of sugar to the coffee.

heal

I hope my fractured leg will **heal** quickly.

heel

The **heel** of his shoe is caught in a crack.

allowed

I'm **allowed** to skateboard on the sidewalk.

aloud

I read my story **aloud** in class.

hall

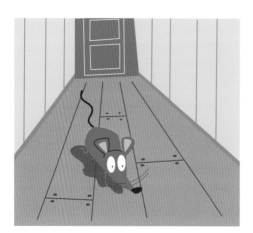

A mouse scurried down the **hall**.

haul

The crane will **haul** the cargo onto the ship.

ant

The **ant** carried my lunch away on his back.

aunt

My **aunt** always pinches my cheek.

hair

The princess let down her golden **hair**.

hare

The **hare** and the tortoise had a race.

ate

A mole **ate** all the plants in the garden.

eight

The dog had a litter of **eight** puppies.

groan

grown

The injured lion's **groan** was loud.

Has my cousin **grown** taller than me?

bald

The sun beamed down on the man's **bald** head.

bawled

The toddler **bawled** when she fell off the swing.

gait

A baby walks with a
wobbly **gait**.

gate

We enter the garden
through the **gate**.

bare

The old lady's cupboard was **bare**.

bear

A famished **bear** searched for berries.

foul

The umpire yelled,
"**Foul** ball!"

fowl

Turkey is the **fowl** we
eat on Thanksgiving.

base

The player was tagged out at second **base**.

bass

The jazz musician played the **bass**.

flour

The muffin recipe calls for one cup of **flour**.

flower

Which is your favorite **flower** in this bouquet?

beat

They danced to the **beat** of the bongo drum.

beet

The farmer had the prize-winning red **beet** at the fair.

flew

flu

The kite **flew** above the trees.

My body aches when I have the **flu**.

berry

bury

The chef placed a **berry** on top of the cake.

My puppy tried to **bury** his big bone.

flea

flee

The **flea** danced on
the dog's back.

He tried to **flee** from
the fiery dragon.

blew

blue

The wind **blew** the papers off the desk.

Robins lay bright **blue** eggs.

fir

Fir trees are green all year round.

fur

The rabbit's **fur** keeps him warm in winter.

board

It's my job to erase the **board** this week.

bored

Sometimes I feel **bored** on a rainy day.

feat

feet

Swimming the channel
was an amazing **feat**.

Keep your **feet** off
the furniture.

bold

bowled

Bold mountain climbers
reached the top.

The girl **bowled** her
first strike.

fair

It isn't **fair** if you have
more than me.

fare

How much is the
bus **fare**?

brake

break

I use my **brake** to stop when I ride my bike.

Be careful not to **break** the crystal vase.

ewe

The **ewe** followed her
wandering lamb.

you

Will **you** help me
tie my shoe?

bridal

Her **bridal** gown was made of satin and lace.

bridle

The cowboy placed the **bridle** on the horse.

earn

I **earn** extra money delivering newspapers.

urn

The archaeologist found an ancient **urn**.

buy

I'll use my allowance to **buy** chocolates for mom.

by

We stood **by** the fountain to make a wish.

doe

The **doe** watched over her fawn.

dough

We roll the **dough** to make a piecrust.

carat

carrot

The queen wore a ten-**carat** diamond ring.

The rabbit stole a **carrot** from the garden.

die

I was sad to see my
goldfish **die**.

dye

My mom let me **dye**
my hair blue.

ceiling

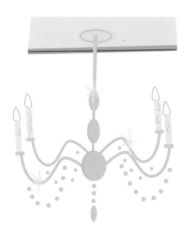

A beautiful chandelier hung from the **ceiling**.

sealing

Mine

The workers are **sealing** the dangerous mine.

dear

My grandparents are
very **dear** to me.

deer

The **deer** ran through
the woods at dusk.

cell

The prisoner was locked in his **cell**.

sell

We **sell** lemonade on a hot summer day.

days

How many **days** are left until vacation?

daze

I was in a **daze** after I bumped my head.

cellar

We slowly creep down the stairs to the **cellar**.

seller

The book **seller** has many novels for me to read.

close

Close the window
before it rains.

clothes

Happy New Year

We bought new **clothes**
for the holidays.

chews

The cow lazily **chews** the grass.

choose

Which game will you **choose** to play?

chili

chilly

Chili peppers are really spicy.

It begins to get **chilly** in the autumn.

Index

Index (continued)

Index (continued)

Index (continued)

Index (continued)

Index (continued)

eye like®

A series to See, Learn, and Grow
Open a child's eyes to the vivid impact of the natural world

ISBN – 13: 978-1-60214-041-7

Play Bac Publishing USA, Inc.
225 Varick Street
New York, NY 10014-4381

Printed in Malaysia

Distributed by
Black Dog & Leventhal Publishers, Inc.
151 West 19th Street
New York, NY 10011

First printing, April 2008